I0818560

WNBA

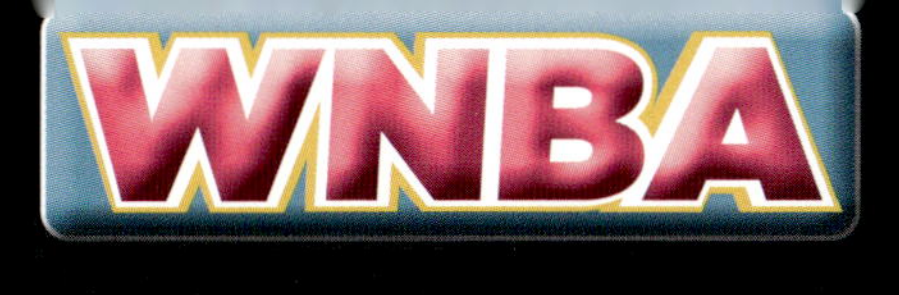

INDIANA FEVER

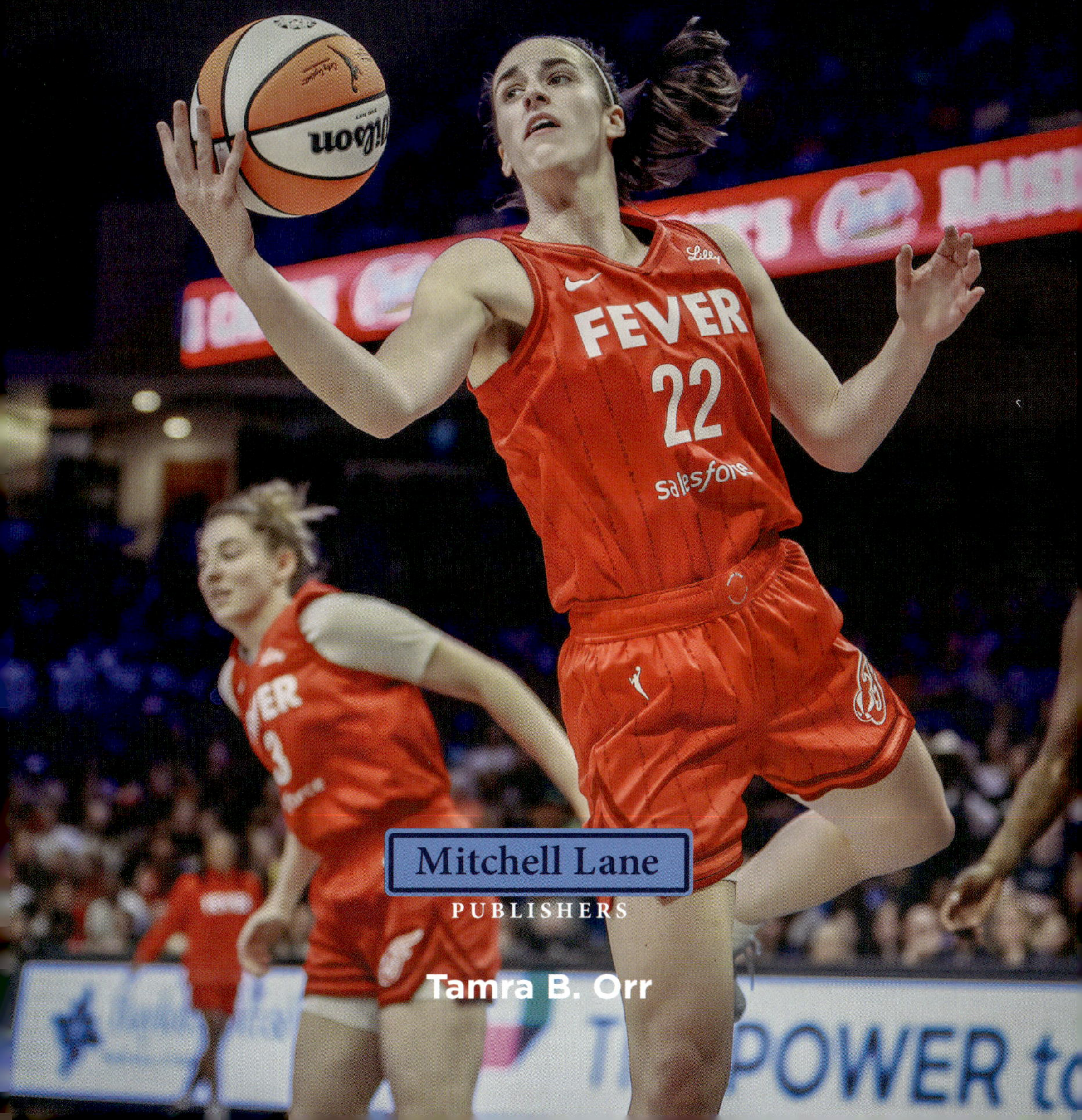

Mitchell Lane
PUBLISHERS

Tamra B. Orr

Mitchell Lane
PUBLISHERS

mitchelllanepub.com

2001 SW 31st Avenue
Hallandale, FL 33009

First Edition, 2026.
Author: Tamra B. Orr
Designer: Ed Morgan
Editor: Tammy Gagne

Series: WNBA
Title: Indiana Fever

Library bound ISBN: 979-8-89260-479-6
eBook ISBN: 979-8-89260-493-2

Photo credits: p. 11 SportsLogos.net; p. 15 wikimedia; Alamy, freepik.com

CONTENTS

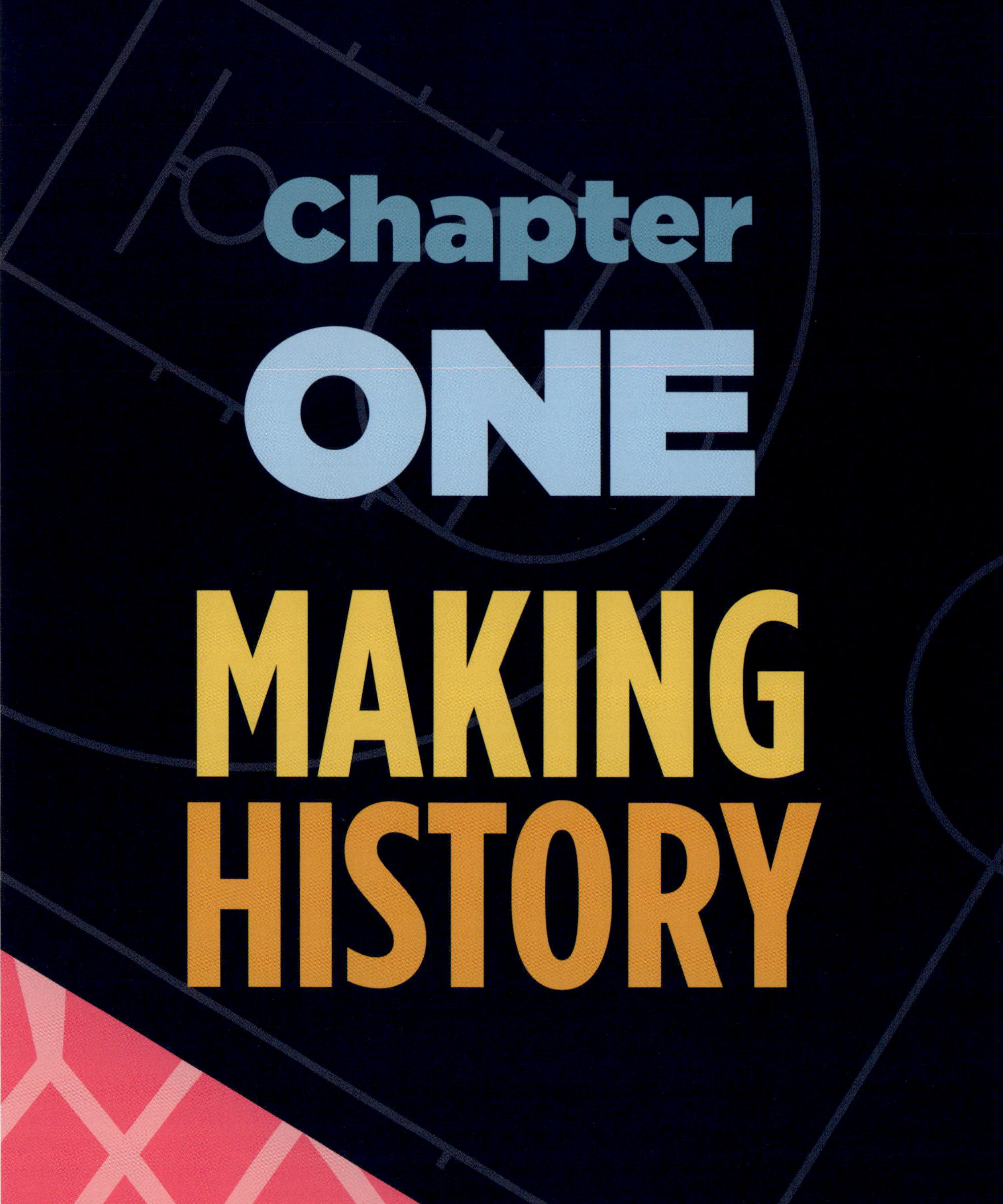

Chapter ONE

MAKING HISTORY

Caitlin Clark's moves on the court often surprise other players, such as DiJonai Carrington (right) in this game against the Sun.

The Indiana Fever had lost to the New York Liberty nine times in a row. That was not surprising. Liberty was one of the strongest teams in the Women's National Basketball Association (WNBA). However, on July 6, 2024, that was about to change, thanks to a **rookie** named Caitlin Clark.

CHAPTER ONE

Every basketball player has strengths and weaknesses. Some players are best at long jump shots. Some players can race in, seeming to capture every **rebound**. Still others excel at passing the ball to the best position to sink the shot. And then there is Clark. As a guard for the Indiana Fever, she proves that, now and then, a player comes along who is good at almost everything.

During the Fever versus Liberty game, Clark was everywhere. Her shots arced over the court and swooshed through the net, winning the game 83–78. By the time the final buzzer rang, Clark had scored an amazing 19 points and racked up 13 **assists** and 12 rebounds. Achieving double digits in three categories such as these is known as a triple-double. It is an incredibly rare accomplishment. It is even rarer when you realize that Clark was a rookie. This triple-double by a rookie was the first in the WNBA's history.

FAST FACT

Caitlin Clark won three gold medals while representing the United States in international basketball competitions between 2017 and 2021.

After the win, Clark told ESPN, "I take a lot of pride in being able to do a lot of different things for this team. I think we're really good when I can get the ball off the glass and just go in **transition** and find my teammates and set them up."

Christie Sides was the Fever's coach for the 2024 season. She was certainly pleased with her newest player. "Caitlin with a triple-double, my gosh, that's incredible," she told ESPN.

Clark possesses an obvious talent for the game. Still, she remains humble. While discussing the triple-double in an interview with *USA Today*, she said simply, "I guess it was really cool."

Making History

Coach Sides (left) watches the court action alongside Clark. The rookie was a great addition to the Indiana Fever.

Chapter TWO

BECOMING THE FEVER

Naming a professional sports team isn't easy. Teams want a name that is easy to remember yet powerful. Some fans wonder how the Indiana Fever came up with their name. They chose the word *fever* because it means "excitement." This is what they wanted their fans to feel when watching games.

CHAPTER TWO

Choosing a mascot can also be tricky. The Indiana Fever's mascot is bright red, furry, and very huggable. Freddy Fever first appeared in June 2000 at the Fever's first home game. At each game, Freddy dresses in his own team jersey and explodes onto the court. Sometimes he rides a scooter or a motorcycle. He also dances, juggles, and shoots the ball. No matter what, he keeps the crowd laughing.

Home games for the Fever are held at Gainbridge Fieldhouse in Indianapolis. This arena can hold more than 18,000 fans. It has been named the best sports facility in the United States multiple times. One of the fans' favorite features is the arena's excellent **sightlines** from almost every seat in the house.

Becoming the Fever

Two of the Fever's guards, Layshia Clarendon and Shavonte Zellous, wait for a game to get started.

FAST FACT

The Indiana Fever joined the WNBA in 1999.

CHAPTER TWO

Like many other teams, Indiana Fever enjoys giving back to the community. In 2023, Caitlin Clark took part in Gainbridge's 1001 Hours of Impact project. During the event, she tossed basketballs with young players and volunteers to raise money for Habitat for Humanity.

Kelsey Mitchell, a Fever guard, has won several awards for her community work in both Indianapolis and her hometown of Cincinnati, Ohio. Mitchell's organization, the Kelz Hoops Foundation, holds backpack and toy drives, which help pay sports fees for high school students. In an interview on the Fever's website, WNBA **Commissioner** Cathy Engelbert stated, "Kelsey's work with young people and families in her community continues to make an enormous positive influence. Along with her fellow WNBA players, Kelsey is dedicated to making the world a better place for the next generation."

Becoming the Fever

Kelsey Mitchell is one of the Fever's best players—plus she works hard to give back to her community.

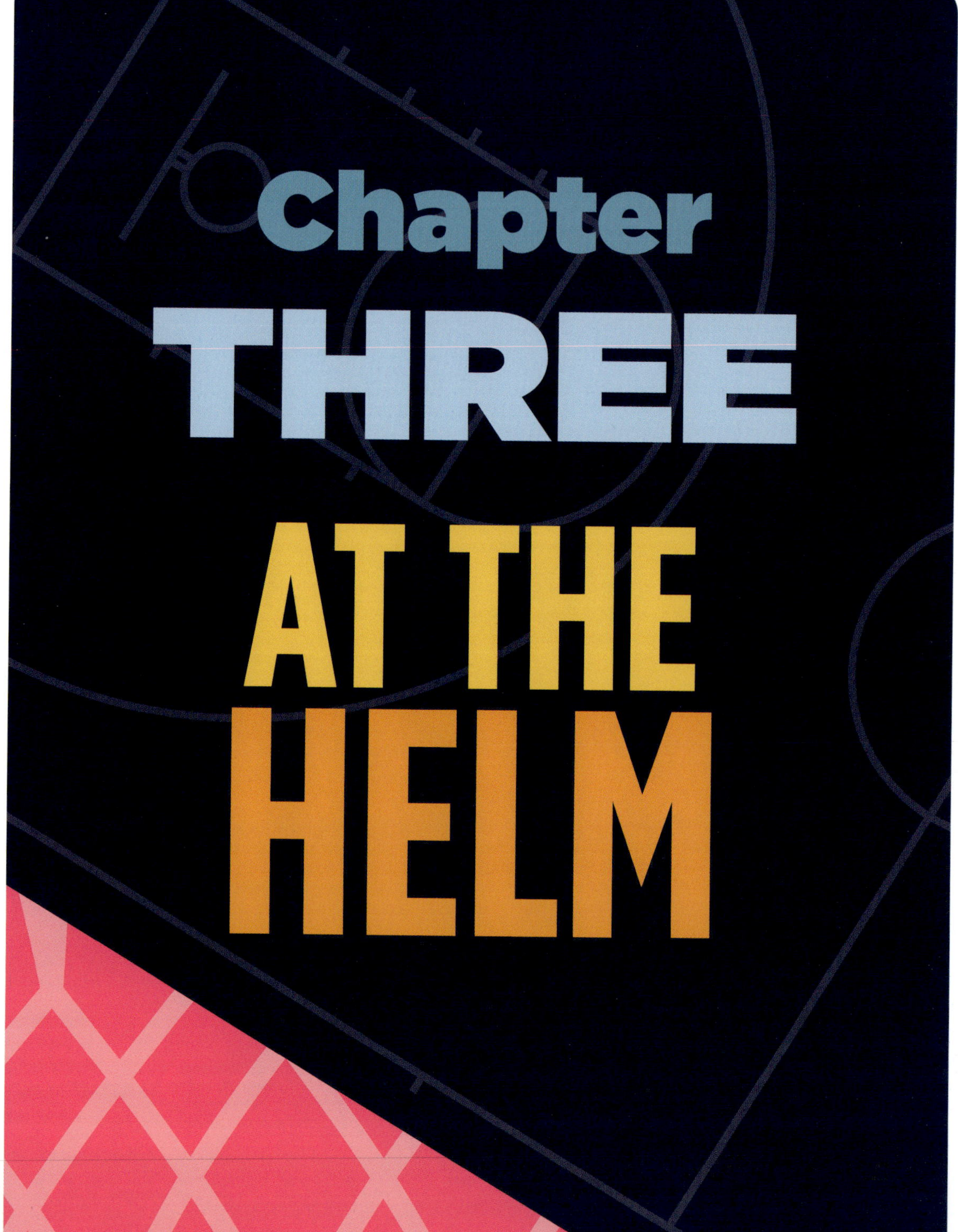

Chapter THREE

AT THE HELM

Christie Sides has been passionate about basketball for more than twenty years.

The journey from working as an assistant coach in a Louisiana high school to becoming the head coach of the Indiana Fever was a busy one for Christie Sides. Over twenty years, she moved up and up until she became an assistant coach to the Fever in 2017. She remained in this role for two years. Then in 2022, she was named head coach.

CHAPTER THREE

Sides knew the game of basketball from the inside. She played the guard position in college, so she understands exactly what it feels like to be on the court, handling the ball. She later coached college teams, including Louisiana State University's Lady Tigers. She was also an assistant coach for the WNBA's Chicago Sky. Sides even coached the Russian Spartak Moscow team all the way to EuroLeague Women's championships.

Sides was excited about coaching the Fever's great players. Always seeing their potential, she wanted to help them play their absolute best. Sides's time as head coach came to an end after two years in this role. Upon departing, she told *Sports Illustrated*, "Leave it better than you found it." She had indeed done this. In 2024, the Fever made it into the playoffs for the first time since 2016.

At the Helm

FAST FACT

Christie Sides played basketball on two college teams, Louisiana State University and the University of Louisiana at Monroe.

CHAPTER THREE

Following the 2024 season, former Fever coach Stephanie White returned to Indiana. She had entered the record books in 2015 when the Fever went all the way to the WNBA Finals. Although the team lost the championship to the Minnesota Lynx, it was the first time a rookie coach had ever led a team to the finals. White hopes to bring the Fever back to the playoffs in the future.

At the Helm

Stephanie White

The Fever's players said goodbye to Christie Sides, and welcomed a familiar face with Stephanie White.

Chapter FOUR

AT THE TOP

Every year, the WNBA holds a draft to choose new players. Teams take turns selecting promising young athletes for the upcoming season. The Fever drafted NaLyssa Smith in 2022 with the second overall pick that year. She became a valuable player for Indiana. She was a starting player in every game of her first season with the team. As a **forward**, she regularly contributed to both the team's offense and defense.

CHAPTER FOUR

Aliyah Boston was the number one overall draft pick in 2023. A forward and **center**, Aliyah Boston was named Rookie of the Year that season. Boston began playing basketball when she was just nine years old and living in the Virgin Islands. After playing for the University of South Carolina, she moved to the Fever. She has since become one of the team's strongest players.

On April 15, 2024, almost 2.5 million people, a new record, tuned in to watch the WNBA Draft on television. Many viewers wanted to see where the record-breaking Caitlin Clark would end up. The twenty-two-year-old had already gained many fans as a star player for the University of Iowa's Hawkeyes. When she was chosen by Indiana Fever, it was truly a dream come true for her. "This is something I wrote down on a piece of paper when I was in . . . second grade," she said in a *People* magazine interview.

FAST FACT

At 6 feet, 5 inches (1.96 m), Boston is the tallest Indiana Fever player.

CHAPTER FOUR

She has been everything Fever coaches, players, and fans hoped she would be. Clark averaged an amazing 17.1 points per game in 2024. She also averaged 5.8 rebounds and 8.2 assists. At the end of the 2024 season, Clark was named WNBA Rookie of the Year. She received 66 of the 67 votes for the award.

Clark and the rest of the Indiana Fever players are ready to keep the team winning on and off the court. After finishing 2024 with a record of 20–20, they hope to do even better in the upcoming seasons. You can bet **Hoosiers**—and many others—will be watching!

At the Top

With Clark at their side, the Indiana Fever players know that they have an exciting future ahead of them.

GLOSSARY

assists
Passes made to teammates which lead to scored points

center
A basketball player who plays near the basket, often the tallest member of the team

commissioner
The chief executive of a sports league such as the WNBA

forward
A basketball player who plays near the basket, often rebounding and scoring goals

Hoosiers
A nickname for people who live in the state of Indiana

rebound
A caught basketball after a missed shot

rookie
An athlete playing her first season as a member of a professional sports team

sightlines
Views of a game from stadium seats

transition
A phase in which an athlete shifts from defensive to offensive play

SLAM DUNK WNBA TRIVIA

- The Indiana Fever played its first game on May 31, 2000, beating the Miami Sol, 57–54.
- Fans of the team are known as Fever Nation.
- The team made it into the WNBA Finals in 2009, 2012, and 2015.
- The Fever won its first and only championship in 2012.
- The Fever retired Tamika Catchings' jersey number, 24, in 2017.
- Aliyah Boston joined the team in 2023. She was selected as the first overall draft pick that year.

FIND OUT MORE

IN PRINT

Anderson, Josh. *Indiana Fever*. Lerner Publications, 2025.

Chandler, Matt. *Caitlin Clark: Basketball Phenom*. Capstone Press, 2025.

Mooney, Carla. *New York Liberty*. Mitchell Lane Publishers, 2026.

ON THE INTERNET

Indiana Fever.
https://fever.wnba.com.

"Indiana Fever," *ESPN*, n.d.
www.espn.com/wnba/team/_/name/ind/indiana-fever.

"Indiana Fever," *FOX Sports*, n.d.
www.foxsports.com/wnba/indiana-fever-team.

INDEX

About the Author

Tamra B. Orr is a full-time writer and author living in the Pacific Northwest. She grew up in Indiana and was one of the many fans who couldn't wait for basketball season to start. Even though she lives a long way from her home state now, she still keeps an eye on Hoosier sports. After graduating from Ball State University in Muncie, Orr began writing and hasn't stopped since. She is a wife, mom, grandma, and avid reader.